HUMAN RESOURCE MANAGEMENT IN THE FUTURE

10 Emerging Trends in HRM

Calvine Odero

Copyright © 2022 Calvine Odhiambo Odero

All rights reserved

The characters and events portrayed in this book are fictitious. Any similarity to real persons, living or dead, is coincidental and not intended by the author.

No part of this book may be reproduced, or stored in a retrieval system, or transmitted in any form or by any means, electronic, mechanical, photocopying, recording, or otherwise, without express written permission of the publisher.

ISBN: 9798831171815
Imprint: Independently published

Printed in the United States of America

I dedicate the discussion to Human Resource professionals offering HRM services in the competitive global business environment.

I am convinced that nothing we do is more important than hiring and developing people. At the end of the day, you bet on people not on strategies

LAWRENCE BOSSIDY

CONTENTS

Title Page
Copyright
Dedication
Epigraph
HOW WILL HRM LOOK IN THE FUTURE? — 1
1. Evolution of Recruitment — 2
2. Collaboration Takes Center Stage — 3
3. Employee Retention — 4
4. HR Professionals Become Strategic Partners — 5
5. HR Meets Big Data — 6
6. Innovation and Automation Makes HR More Efficient — 7
7. HR Becomes Even More Important — 8
8. HR Focuses on Diversity and Inclusion — 9
9. HR Embraces Artificial Intelligence — 10
10. HR Prioritizes Brand Loyalty — 11
CONCLUSION — 12
REFERENCES — 13
About The Author — 15
Books By This Author — 17
— 19

HOW WILL HRM LOOK IN THE FUTURE?

The answer to this question depends largely on where you work today, your company's culture, and whether you can adapt to an ever-changing business landscape. However, there are several trends that are influencing how HR departments operate today, and these are likely to continue into the future. To help you get an idea of what Human Resource Management in the future might look like, here is an outline of key trends currently shaping the way businesses manage their employees and prepare for their own futures. You might be surprised at just how different things will be in 10 years!

1. EVOLUTION OF RECRUITMENT

The evolution of HR's role within organizations will be most noticeable when you look at how employee recruitment has evolved over time. Human Resources was responsible for recruiting new employees, but today it's a partnership between human resources and marketing, since recruiting is often just one aspect of effective branding (Hussain, Channa & Bhutto, 2022). In fact, marketers are responsible for a significant proportion of new hires - and they're expected to become more involved with recruitment as time goes on.

2. COLLABORATION TAKES CENTER STAGE

HR departments have historically been siloed from other departments, working independently from each other. But those days are long gone. Instead, HR professionals need to be able to collaborate across teams and departments, particularly when it comes to making sure your company's benefits package is competitive. You also need to keep an eye out for emerging technologies that could change your industry (and therefore affect your company). For example, advances in automation could dramatically change employment practices - and companies will need smart HR professionals who can help them adapt. Finally, think about what kind of culture you want to create within your organization: Is it important that everyone feel included? Or do you value efficiency above all else? (Watson, 2022). These are all questions you should consider before writing your HR plan.

3. EMPLOYEE RETENTION

One thing won't change in HR planning over time: employee retention will always be a top priority. If your team isn't happy, they won't work well together - which means low productivity and high turnover rates. That said, there may be different ways to approach retention in 10 years than there were 10 years ago. Today, many companies offer perks like free meals or paid parental leave to attract talent; but tomorrow? They might offer even more unique perks, such as telecommuting opportunities or flexible hours so workers can manage their personal lives better (Kumar, 2022). Keep an eye out for these kinds of changes so you can incorporate them into your HR strategy accordingly!

4. HR PROFESSIONALS BECOME STRATEGIC PARTNERS

As mentioned earlier, HR professionals used to focus mainly on administrative tasks and day-to-day operations. Nowadays, however, HR professionals are increasingly strategic partners whose input is valued by C-level executives, especially when it comes to developing strategies for retaining key talent. At its core, HR planning focuses on helping businesses run smoothly and effectively (Hamid, Muzamil & Shah, 2022). And while there's no way to predict exactly how HR will evolve in the future, one thing is certain: Businesses need strong leaders who understand not only how to write a business plan but also how to implement it strategically.

5. HR MEETS BIG DATA

Big data is a term that refers to massive amounts of information, and it's something that HR professionals will need to get comfortable with in order to succeed. Why? Because big data can be used to make predictions about everything from employee behavior to market trends (Yang, 2022). HR departments will likely play a huge role in collecting and analyzing all of that information, which will allow them to make smarter decisions moving forward.

6. INNOVATION AND AUTOMATION MAKES HR MORE EFFICIENT

As technology continues to advance at a rapid pace, you'll need all of your employees - not just your most experienced ones - to be creative and innovative. To achieve that goal, you'll need to make sure that every member of your company embraces new ideas in the work environment. Already, some HR departments are using automated software programs for routine tasks like payroll and benefits administration. As time goes on, you can expect to see more and more HR software that automates tasks like recruitment and employee evaluation (Elayan et al., 2022). That's good news for HR professionals who are looking for ways to save time, but it also means you'll need to be prepared to spend a lot of time learning new software programs.

7. HR BECOMES EVEN MORE IMPORTANT

When it comes down to it, Human Resources is all about people - and as long as there are people in your company, Human Resources will be an essential part of your business plan. No matter how advanced technology becomes or how automated processes streamline your workflow, you'll still need HR professionals who can make sure your employees are engaged and productive (Torre, Sarti & Antonelli, 2022). And as long as people are a crucial part of your business, human resources will remain an integral part of your HR planning.

8. HR FOCUSES ON DIVERSITY AND INCLUSION

Diversity is a hot topic in HR today, and it's one that will continue to be relevant in years to come. The truth is, diversity doesn't just make companies more interesting; it also makes them more innovative. As technology continues to advance at a rapid pace, you'll need all of your employees - not just your most experienced ones - to be creative and innovative (Davis, Dupree & Meltzer, 2022). To achieve that goal, you'll need to make sure that every member of your company feels welcome as part of the team.

9. HR EMBRACES ARTIFICIAL INTELLIGENCE

In recent years, Artificial Intelligence (AI) has become a buzzword in business. And as it turns out, AI will have a major impact on HR planning over time. The reason? It can be used to make more accurate predictions about everything from employee retention to job performance (Charlwood & Guenole, 2022). As a HR professional, you'll need to stay up-to-date on all of AI's latest developments so you can use it to your advantage when planning for your company's future.

10. HR PRIORITIZES BRAND LOYALTY

As a Human Resources professional, you'll be in charge of overseeing relationships between vendors and customers - and that means your department will have an impact on every aspect of your business plan. In fact, your department will be responsible for maintaining relationships with vendors, building partnerships with customers, and creating brand loyalty (Mittal, Gupta & Mottiani, 2022). As you can imagine, that's a tall order - but it's also an exciting opportunity to expand your role in your company.

CONCLUSION

In the past, HRM has been used to measure the efficiency of tasks and people. The concept of efficiency is changing in the modern workforce. Because of this, HRM is changing to enhance measures of happiness, satisfaction, and engagement of the staff. While these measures are not part of the traditional HRM model, they are necessary for improving the motivation, performance, and loyalty of the current and future workforce.

REFERENCES

Charlwood, A., & Guenole, N. (2022). Can HR adapt to the paradoxes of artificial intelligence?. *Human Resource Management Journal.*

Davis, M. A., Dupree, C. H., & Meltzer, C. C. (2022). Diversity, Equity, and Inclusion Efforts Are Organizational Change Management Efforts. *Journal of the American College of Radiology, 19*(1), 181-183.

Elayan, M. B., Hayajneh, J. A. M., Abdellatif, M. A. M., & Abubakar, A. M. (2022). Knowledge-based HR practices, π-shaped skills and innovative performance in the contemporary organizations. *Kybernetes.*

Hamid, Z., Muzamil, M., & Shah, S. A. (2022). Strategic human resource management. In *Research Anthology on Human Resource Practices for the Modern Workforce* (pp. 1-16). IGI Global.

Hussain, T., Channa, K. A., & Bhutto, M. H. (2022). Impact of recruitment practices on organizational commitment: mediating role of employer image. *Journal of Economic and Administrative Sciences.*

Kumar, S. (2022). The impact of talent management practices on employee turnover and retention intentions. *Global Business and Organizational Excellence, 41*(2), 21-34.

Mittal, S., Gupta, V., & Mottiani, M. (2022). Examining the linkages between employee brand love, affective commitment, positive word-of-mouth, and turnover intentions: A social identity theory perspective. *IIMB Management Review*.

Torre, T., Sarti, D., & Antonelli, G. (2022). People Analytics and The Future of Competitiveness: Which Capabilities HR Departments Need to Succeed in the "Next Normal". In *HR Analytics and Digital HR Practices* (pp. 1-24). Palgrave Macmillan, Singapore.

Watson, A. (2022). How organisations can remove barriers to increase workforce collaboration. *Strategic HR Review*.

Yang, H. (2022). Human Resource Big Data Analysis and Decision Making of Group Enterprises Based on Cloud Platform. In *2022 14th International Conference on Measuring Technology and Mechatronics Automation (ICMTMA)* (pp. 1068-1071). IEEE.

ABOUT THE AUTHOR

Calvine Odero

Education: Human Resource Management
Professional Membership: Institute of Human Resource Management (IHRM)
Career: Human Resource Officer

BOOKS BY THIS AUTHOR

Human Resource Management And Development (Hrm&D): A Guide For Hr Students, Interns, And Entry-Level Professionals

The book targets Human Resource Management students, interns, and professionals.

It explains the concepts of Human Resource Management (HRM) and Human Resource Development (HRD).

HRM involves the planning and implementation of HR functions in the organization.

HRD entails regular capacity building to improve the motivation and competencies of the staff.

The discussion enables the target audience to understand the effective and efficient management of the workforce in the competitive business environment.

www.ingramcontent.com/pod-product-compliance
Lightning Source LLC
Chambersburg PA
CBHW050329220526
45465CB00005B/2198